Po
a

Population growth and
migration

363.
9

1775144

Series Editor

Lisa Firth

 Independence

Educational Publishers

D0432753

First published by Independence

The Studio, High Green

Great Shelford

Cambridge CB22 5EG

England

© Independence 2012

Photocopy licence

The material in this book is protected by copyright. However, the
purchaser is free to make multiple copies of particular articles for instructional
purposes for immediate use within the purchasing institution.
Making copies of the entire book is not permitted.

British Library Cataloguing in Publication Data

Population growth and migration. -- (Issues ; v. 220)

1. Population. 2. Emigration and immigration--Social

aspects. 3. Population policy.

I. Series II. Firth, Lisa.

363.9-dc23

363-9

1775144

ISBN-13: 978 1 86168 605 3

Printed in Great Britain

MWL Print Group Ltd

CONTENTS

Chapter 1 Population Pressure

Chapter 2 Migration Trends

OTHER TITLES IN THE ISSUES SERIES

For more on these titles, visit: www.independence.co.uk

A note on critical evaluation

Because the information reprinted here is from a number of different sources, readers should bear in mind the origin of the text and whether the source is likely to have a particular bias when presenting information (just as they would if undertaking their own research). It is hoped that, as you read about the many aspects of the issues explored in this book, you will critically evaluate the information presented. It is important that you decide whether you are being presented with facts or opinions. Does the writer give a biased or an unbiased report? If an opinion is being expressed, do you agree with the writer?

Population Growth and Migration offers a useful starting point for those who need convenient access to information about the many issues involved. However, it is only a starting point. Following each article is a URL to the relevant organisation's website, which you may wish to visit for further information.

The world at seven billion

Even though the world population growth rate has slowed from 2.1 per cent per year in the late 1960s to 1.2 per cent today, the size of the world's population has continued to increase – from five billion in 1987 to six billion in 1999, and to seven billion in 2011.

By Carl Haub and James Gribble

The sixth billion and seventh billion were each added in record time – only 12 years. If the 2.1 per cent growth rate from the 1960s had held steady, world population would be 8.7 billion today. It is entirely possible that the 8th billion will be added in 12 years as well, placing us squarely in the middle of history's most rapid population expansion.

This prospect seems to run counter to the prevailing belief that concern over population growth is a thing of the past, and that today's 'population problem' is that birth rates are too low, not too high. In fact, there is some truth to that notion, depending on the region or country one is talking about. Today, most population growth is concentrated in the world's poorest countries – and within the poorest regions of those countries.

The decrease in the world growth rate since the 1960s resulted from the realisation on the part of some developing-country governments and donors about unprecedented rates of population growth. It took all of human history to reach a world population of 1.6 billion at the beginning of the 20th century. Just 100 years later, in 2000, the population total had reached 6.1 billion. How did this sudden, momentous change come about? To understand this change, we must first consider the demographic transition – the shifts in birth and death rates that historically have occurred over long periods of time. And then we must look at how very differently the transition has taken place in the world's developed and developing countries.

It took all of human history to reach a world population of 1.6 billion at the beginning of the 20th century. Just 100 years later, in 2000, the population total had reached 6.1 billion

The transition describes two trends: the decline in birth rates as the need or desire for larger numbers of children diminished, and the decline in death rates as public health initiatives and modern medicine lengthened life.

In today's developed countries, this transition took many centuries, but in today's developing countries the changes are taking place in mere decades. In developed countries, birth and death rates tended to decline in parallel. Economies and societies changed during that time: fewer families stayed on farms and the Industrial Revolution changed the way people lived and worked. But the transition's pace was still slow. In Sweden, for example, the slowly declining death and birth rates produced a population growth rate that has remained fairly stable over the past 250 years, rarely exceeding one per cent per year.

.TOO HEALTHY..??.

In developing countries during the 20th century, major improvements in public health, the practice of modern medicine, and immunisation campaigns spread quickly, particularly after World War II. Death rates dropped while birth rates stayed high. In Sri Lanka, infant mortality (under age one) in the early 1950s is estimated to have been about 105 deaths per 1,000 live births. By the 1990s, the rate had dropped dramatically to below 20, due in large part to basic public health interventions such as immunisations, oral re-hydration therapy and birth spacing – all of which have contributed to lower rates of infant and child mortality.

With health conditions improving so rapidly, birth rates in developing countries did not have time to change as they did in Europe. This lag between the drop in death rates and the drop in birth rates produced unprecedented levels of population growth. In Kenya, infant mortality declined first – contributing to a rise in life expectancy at birth from about 42 years in the early 1950s to 56 years in the late 1970s – before fertility began a decline from the then-prevalent eight children per woman. During that same period, Kenya's annual population growth rate approached an unheard-of four per cent. In the early 1950s, Pakistan had a life expectancy of 41 years and an average fertility rate of 6.6 children per woman. It was not until the early 1980s, when life expectancy had reached 59 years – due in large part to reductions in infant and child deaths – that Pakistan's fertility began to decrease and its population growth rate began to slow. These lengthy growth spurts resulted in the relatively new phenomenon of government policies aimed at lowering birth rates. Some governments, such as Indonesia and Thailand, were quite successful in lowering birth rates; many other governments have not been.

In addition to policies, social norms also contribute to how a country moves through the demographic transition. Although at times these norms conflict with public policies and programmes, cultural factors such as age at marriage, desired family size and gender roles all have a strong influence on fertility behaviour.

What might the future look like? It is fundamental to remember that all population projections, whether performed by a national statistical office, the United Nations or the US Census Bureau, are based on assumptions. Demographers make assumptions on the future course of the factors that determine population growth or decline: the birth rate and the death rate. When looking at projections, one needs to consider the assumptions before the results. In the case of developing countries, a typical assumption is that birth and death rates will follow the path of demographic transition from high birth and death rates to low ones – mirroring the transition as it played out in developed countries. But when, how and whether that actually happens cannot be known. When considering a population projection for a developing country, several questions need to be posed. If fertility has not yet begun to decline significantly, when will it begin and why? This question would be appropriate for Niger and Uganda, whose fertility rates are still very high at 7.0 and 6.4, respectively. If fertility is declining, will it continue to do so or 'stall' for a time at some lower level as it has in Jordan and Kenya? Finally, will a country's fertility really fall to as little as two children per woman or fewer, as is commonly expected?

July 2011

⇨ The above information is an extract from the Population Reference Bureau's *Population Bulletin: The World at 7 Billion*, and is reprinted with permission. Visit www.prb.org for more information.

© Population Reference Bureau

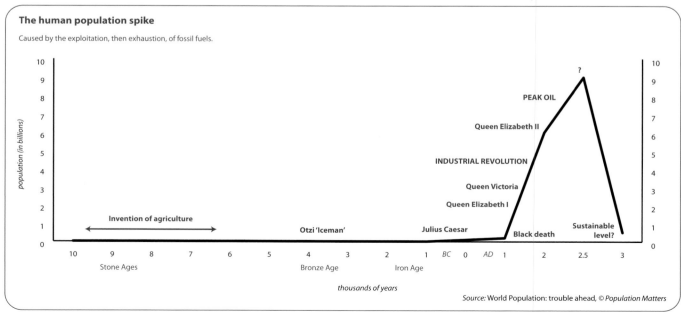

The human population spike

Caused by the exploitation, then exhaustion, of fossil fuels.

Source: World Population: trouble ahead, © *Population Matters*

Population growth

Information from Politics.co.uk

What is population growth?

The human population of Earth has been growing since prehistoric times, but the past 200 years have seen human numbers grow exponentially.

In 1 AD, the world's population was believed to have been around 150 million. By the year 1000, it was still below 300 million, and it was not until around 1830 that global population topped one billion.

The world's population in 2004 stood at an estimated 6.35 billion; more than twice what it was just 40 years ago. While this is expected by many to rise to around eight billion by 2020, United Nations demographic studies point to a declining rate of growth, with the peak occurring between around 1985 and 1990, when population grew by around 87 million per year.

There are widespread concerns about the implications of population growth for the world, in terms of the availability of resources, damage to the environment and the sustainability of social and economic development.

Today, many parts of the developed world have a low, zero or even negative population growth rate. In the post-war era, the population of the developing world, by contrast, has boomed, and between 2000 and 2030, many demographers anticipate virtually all of world population growth to occur in poorer countries, exacerbating these concerns.

Background

Having grown steadily but slowly in previous centuries, the human population's growth rate was transformed for ever by Europe's Agricultural Revolution of the 1700s and the Industrial Revolution of the 1800s. As well as giving birth to the 'modern' world, the dawning of the 'scientific' worldview in this era permitted the production of more food than had ever been possible, the manufacturing of the necessities of life for less than ever before, and significant breakthroughs in medicine, resulting in a plummeting death rate.

Although there had been population spurts in previous centuries, the Industrial Revolution was the first time when this was followed by economic growth, not mass starvation or disease as occurred during the Black Death in the 14th century.

Although Asia had always been, and remains today, home to more than half of the world's population, by 1800, Europeans comprised over a fifth of the world's population, and by 1900, that had risen to almost one quarter.

In the post-war era, however, booming fertility rates – even in the face of high mortality – have seen the developing world become the driving force behind population growth. By 2000, Europe contributed only around 12 per cent of the world's population.

Demographers point to a phenomenon called the 'demographic transition', whereby fertility tends to decline as socio-economic development progresses. Particularly important elements of development in this regard are reproductive health and child health and education improvements. This tends to bring the average number of children per woman towards the 'replacement level', which is calculated at around 2.1. Some countries today are not reaching this level: a number of former Soviet republics, including Russia, have seen a declining population as a result of low fertility and rising mortality.

Much of the developed world has gone through this demographic transition, and those parts of the developing world that have undergone the most development have also experienced substantial drops in fertility (e.g. South Korea, Singapore, Bangladesh, Colombia, etc.). Since 1969, the work of the UN Population Fund (UNFPA) has promoted reproductive health in the developing world, having a significant effect on both fertility and mortality.

Nonetheless, the average fertility rate in the developing world remains higher than three, and as the absolute number of people of reproductive age increases, a slowing in the population growth rate need not actually signal a falling in absolute numbers by which the population grows.

Controversies

The dangers of local overpopulation have long been understood. In a world where geographical mobility was limited and the majority lived at subsistence level, the result of food production falling below the demands put upon it by the population – whether by the failure of the crops or by an excessive birth rate – was starvation. With a soaring population and migration off the land caused by industrialisation, fears that Britain was approaching this were expressed famously in 1798 by Thomas Malthus, whose *Essay on the Principle of Population as it Affects the Future Improvement of Society* warned that food production, which relied on finite factors of production, could not keep up with exponential human reproduction.

Nonetheless, since that time the rate of growth in food productivity has continued to outstrip population growth in absolute terms. Optimistic theorists have argued that technology growth will permit this trend to continue at least until the population reaches ten billion – although this claim is heavily contested.

POLITICS.CO.UK

It is nonetheless the case that famine and poverty continue to exist in a world whose resources, if divided equally amongst all, could support the current population level. Large-scale global redistribution of wealth and resources, however, is a proposition that would pose an enormous challenge to the prevailing world order, and is naturally unattractive to the 'haves'.

Population growth is nonetheless widely regarded as a contributing factor to a number of other problems besides the threat of overpopulation. 70 per cent of deforestation worldwide is directly caused by population growth. As human numbers increase, natural habitats are destroyed. Population growth can therefore cause a deficiency in food, water and forested areas that are important for the world's survival. As population grows, consumption needs increase which causes greater poverty. More people use more energy, release more greenhouse gases and increase global warming.

Furthermore, the poor reproductive health that has accompanied population growth in many parts of the developing world is producing an HIV/AIDS epidemic of massive proportions. Religious and ideological barriers are frequently accused of standing in the way of improving reproductive health and stemming population growth, particularly the opposition of the Roman Catholic Church to birth control and family planning.

Most countries treat reproduction as something that cannot be regulated, but a few do not. China has a well-known 'one-child rule', introduced in 1979, explicitly as a means of controlling population (although it only applies to ethnic Han Chinese living in urban areas). Its effectiveness is widely questioned, and its human rights implications are frequently condemned. Following a devastating earthquake in the country in May 2008, in which thousands of children were killed, Chinese officials announced that parents whose child had been killed, severely injured or disabled, would be allowed to have another child.

Statistics

From 275 million in the late 1960s when the concept of 'least developed' was formulated, Sub-Saharan Africa's population has grown to about 840 million and continues to increase by about 20 million per year. The region has the world's highest fertility, with a regional total fertility rate (TFR) of about 5.1 lifetime births per woman. The UN Population Division forecasts a population of 1.8 billion in 2050. However, that projection is based on the assumption that the use of family planning in all countries will increase and that TFR, on average, would decline to 2.5.

Asia and the Pacific is home to nearly 60 per cent of the world's total population. China, with 1.3 billion people, is the world's largest country. India, with 1.2 billion people, is currently projected to pass China as the world's largest in population at some point between 2020 and 2025. The potential for rapid population growth in India continues as TFRs remain high in many of its most populous states, such as Bihar, Rajasthan and Uttar Pradesh. The possibility of India reaching two billion in population cannot be ruled out.

By 2050, in the absence of immigration, the population of Central and Eastern Europe and Central Asia is expected to have decreased to 394 million and to have aged substantially. The prospects for population decline may be changing in some countries in response to government programmes to encourage childbearing.

As a result of declining fertility, population growth in Latin America and the Caribbean will be comparatively modest between now and 2050, rising to about 730 million by 2050, an increase of 25 per cent.

The Arab countries once had one of the highest population growth rates in the world. Today, the region's growth rate stands at two per cent annually and, with the low TFRs in many countries, it will continue to decrease.

Source: UNFPA – 2011

⇨ The above information is reprinted with kind permission from Politics.co.uk. Visit www.politics.co.uk for more information.

Countries with the highest populations, 1950 and 2010

1950		2010	
China	562,579,779	China	1,347,563,498
India	369,880,000	India	1,184,090,490
USA	152,271,000	USA	309,162,581
Russia	101,936,816	Indonesia	242,968,342
Japan	83,805,000	Brazil	201,103,330
Indonesia	82,978,392	Pakistan	179,659,223
Germany	68,374,572	Bangladesh	159,765,367
Brazil	53,443,075	Nigeria	152,217,341
UK	50,127,000	Russia	139,390,205
Italy	47,105,000	Japan	126,804,433

Source: © GeoHive

POLITICS.CO.UK

Population and human development: the key connections

Concern over the world's booming human population – which has grown from three to nearly seven billion in little more than 40 years – has abated somewhat as birth rates have fallen right across the world. But there is still a long way to go before numbers stabilise at somewhere between eight and 11 billion – and some countries, such as Pakistan and Nigeria, are on course to triple their numbers by the middle of this 21st century.

Globally, many experts are concerned that the Earth's 'carrying capacity' is already overstrained, and worry that the huge impending increases in consumption in countries such as India and China will add enormously to the burden of greenhouse gases which threaten to heat the planet – not to mention all the other demands which increases in both population and consumption are putting on the Earth's natural systems. Indeed, some commentators argue that one of the best strategies for reducing future greenhouse gas emissions is to stabilise population as quickly as can be achieved by non-coercive education and reproductive health programmes.

Nor is the problem confined to the so-called 'developing world'. The United States, for example, produces a quarter of the world's carbon dioxide emissions with only five per cent of the global population. And, unlike Europe, the US population is growing fast – from 200 million in 1970, to over 310 million today [2011] and a projected 420 million in 2050.

Some countries... are on course to triple their numbers by the middle of the 21st century

One of the complicating facts is that much of the world's population – especially in the South – is very young, with plenty of potential to reproduce. So that although the rate of population growth began to decline some 30 years ago, annual additions to the human population are still near to their highest level, with some 75 million being added every year, or over 200,000 people every day. This is the equivalent of a San Francisco every week and almost a Germany every year.

These people all need food, housing, jobs and healthcare. And once basic needs are met, the appetite for other consumer goods and services seems to be limited only by the ability to pay for them. Human impacts on resources and on the environment vary, therefore, not only with changes in population growth and distribution

but also with changes in levels of consumption and the technologies involved.

For example, since 1950 the richest fifth of humanity has doubled its consumption of energy, meat, timber, steel and copper per person and quadrupled its car ownership, while the poorest fifth of humanity has increased its general consumption hardly at all.

Making problems worse

For this reason, booming population is only one among many causes of social and environmental problems. But such growth can make these problems much more difficult to solve. However, for a variety of reasons, including the previous US Government's attitude towards family planning, population has slipped down the international agenda, almost to the point of disappearing. President Obama's swift action to restore funding to the UN Population Fund and rising concern over the impacts of climate change on the Earth's natural resources and food supply, have begun to bring the issue of population back into focus – but much time has been wasted.

Indeed, a report in 2007 from UK parliamentarians said 'a whole decade has been lost' in dealing with the problem. They pointed especially to the rampant growth of human numbers in many poor African countries where the problem of land degradation and poverty are most severe.

Ethiopia, for example, has seen its numbers grow from 42 million at the time of the infamous famine in 1984 to 90 million today. By 2050 its population is projected to reach 145 million – and this at a time when eight million Ethiopians already live on permanent food aid.

In Sub-Saharan Africa, as a whole, the numbers of people in extreme poverty fell from nearly 48 per cent in 1990 to 41.1 per cent by 2004, with most of the progress achieved in the previous seven years. However, the MDG report for 2007 said that what little progress has been made had stalled and that there was no immediate likelihood of further reductions in poverty

Population: assessment of global megatrends

Increasing global divergence in population trends.

> **The main demographic characteristics of this century are expected to be:**
>
> ⇨ ageing of societies, which will spread to most countries;
>
> ⇨ slower global population growth, with major regional differences;
>
> ⇨ migration, especially caused by environmental factors.

Today, the world population is continuing to grow, although much more slowly than in the recent past. It has more than doubled since the 1960s but is very unlikely to double again during the current century (IIASA, 2007). Instead, it is expected to peak at approximately nine billion by around 2050 (UN Population Division, 2009) or 2070 (IIASA, 2007). There is a less than ten per cent chance that in 2100 there will be fewer people than today, or that the total will exceed 11 billion (Lutz et al., 2008).

Considerable differences exist, however, in terms of projected regional population growth. A major decline is forecast in eastern Europe, where the population is expected to be less than half today's level by 2100. Contrastingly, in many African countries the population is likely to have doubled by 2100 (IIASA, 2007).

Demographers expect the average age of populations to rise throughout this century

From 2020–2030 onwards, declining populations are also expected in some developing countries, especially in Asia. Most of the countries of North America and western Europe are still growing despite ageing, mostly due to migration. However, it is expected that they will also register declines if policies are not introduced to compensate for the impacts of advanced ageing; for example, measures to attract migrants.

China can expect a dramatic demographic transformation with a massive shift in age structure. China's population is projected to start declining around 2030 and the working-age population, which currently provides one of the biggest drivers of economic growth, will decline rapidly both in absolute terms and as a proportion of the total population. After initially increasing, by mid-century

China's population will have fallen to its size in 2000 and by the end of the century it may have halved from the 2000 level. China's trends are qualified, however, by considerable uncertainty over expected fertility rates, gender balance (the relative number of baby girls born is declining due to the one-child policy), the population's age structure and the current size of the population (IIASA, 2007).

Demographers expect the average age of populations to rise throughout this century. Particularly rapid increases are foreseen in the next few decades, especially in some developing countries (notably China, some Pacific islands and central Asian states). From about 2030 to 2050, this trend will spread to most regions of the world (Lutz et al., 2008; NIC, 2008).

There are obvious differences between developed and developing countries in terms of the speed of ageing. By 2050, developing countries are expected to be ageing as fast as the developed world is now (Jackson and Howe, 2008). Developing countries will have less time to adapt than developed countries and face challenges in addressing changes in the structure of society with limited resources.

One significant impact of ageing is on the size of the working population. It has already peaked in developed countries and is expected to peak in around 2015 in China (Lutz, 2009; CIA, 2001). The oldest in society are also more vulnerable to disease and climate change impacts, placing new demands on society (CIA, 2001; DG ECFIN, 2009).

In contrast to the marked ageing of many developed world populations, many developing country populations will have substantial 'youth bulges' (disproportionate concentrations of people in the 15- to 29-year-old age group) until 2025. Several of the countries with the largest bulges are located in Sub-Saharan Africa and the Middle East and are among the world's most unstable (or potentially unstable) states.

These demographic differences, combined with growing economic disparities, are increasing the pressure for migration, which is expected to become a more important factor in demographic change over the next 50 years. Environmentally-induced migration will gain in importance. Migration significantly affects ethnic diversity, age composition and the size of the workforce in recipient countries.

While there is reasonable confidence over broad trends in the shorter term, substantial uncertainty attaches to the specific trend for any country or region (NRC, 2001).

After 1950, migration was driven by the liberalisation of trade in goods and by movements of capital, and was further accelerated by differences in income and by conflict. Migration can benefit both host countries, for example by filling a labour gap, and home countries through remittances. Migrations are complex and uncertain phenomena which depend on a range of undefined social, economic and environmental factors. There is currently no way to consider these uncertainties in projections.

Life expectancy rose rapidly in the 20th century, thanks to improvements in public health, nutrition and medicine

From a development perspective, what matters is not simply the number of people in a country but also the population's productive potential or human capital (DRC, 2008). The shifting distribution of human capital (quantified in terms of the people of working age with at least a secondary education) differs from the main demographic trends. Europe and North America possess the most human capital today but in the future Asia is expected to show the biggest gains, with Africa remaining at the bottom. By around 2015, China's human capital will overtake Europe's and North America's combined (Poncet, 2006).

Key drivers and uncertainties

Fertility, mortality, migration, economic development, poverty and governance are the main drivers of population growth. Uncertainty abounds however, for example with respect to migration flows, female education and access to birth control, fertility rates, access to healthcare and life expectancy (NIC, 2008). How will government policies on education, health, migration and urbanisation develop? How will technology improve the lives of elderly people? There is even uncertainty over our current situation, including fertility levels in China and HIV/AIDS prevalence in Africa (IIASA, 2007).

The development of fertility rates in different parts of the world is uncertain, especially after the transition to older societies in developed countries. Half the world already has a fertility rate below the long-term replacement level. That includes all of Europe, and much of the Caribbean and the Far East. Even small changes in fertility rates can lead to significant changes in population sizes. Globally, women today have half as many babies as their mothers did, mostly from choice. The average age at which women have children influences population dynamics.

Concerning mortality, demographers have historically tended to underestimate gains in life expectancy, which has affected population-ageing predictions. New approaches and alternative indicators are being developed to take into account the effect of longer, healthier lives. Uncertainties regarding life expectancy relate to the biological upper limit of the human lifespan (particularly in developed countries) and to the efficiency of local health services (especially in developing countries). Uncertainties also exist regarding how far the positive effects of longer, healthier lives will be cancelled out by other trends such as increased inequalities, decreasing health of poor people and the spread of diseases. The links between ageing and economic growth are now better understood, however, showing that ageing's costs to society may be less than predicted earlier (Pearce, 2010).

Life expectancy rose rapidly in the 20th century, thanks to improvements in public health, nutrition and medicine. It is expected to increase further, supported by technology and economic development and access to healthcare, although the associated costs could restrict many of the benefits to the wealthiest in society. Access to healthcare, clean drinking water, sanitation, family planning services, healthy food and advanced treatment varies and could cause increasing health gaps between rich and poor. These inequalities exist between regions but also within countries and cities, especially in emerging economies (EEA, 2010a).

Poverty is a key driver of migration, which is considered the most uncertain driver of population growth (IIASA, 2007). Economic growth, environmental degradation, climate change impacts and migration policies are the main uncertainties influencing international migration flows.

The increasing uncertainties and complexity in projected demographic trends suggest that existing population forecasting methods are inadequate. With this in mind, it is important that decision-makers relying on scenario studies gain a better understanding of uncertainty and the way that projections are made (Lutz, 2009). To achieve that, uncertainties and assumptions on which projections are based need to be communicated better to users (IIASA, 2007).

Note

A full list of all references cited in this article are available online at: http://www.eea.europa.eu/soer/europe-and-the-world/megatrends/at_download/file

⇨ The above information is an extract from the European Environment Agency's report *State and outlook 2010: assessment of global megatrends*, and is reprinted with permission. Visit www.eea.europa.eu for more information.

© *European Environment Agency*

EUROPEAN ENVIRONMENT AGENCY

'We're already way past the carrying capacity of this planet by a very simple standard,' he says. 'We are not living on the interest from our natural capital – we are living on the capital itself. The working parts of our life support system are going down the drain at thousands of times the rate that has been the norm over the past millions and millions of years.'

You cannot view consumption and population growth as separate issues, says Ehrlich: 'In one sense, it is the consumption that damages our life support system as opposed to the actual number of people expanding. But both multiply together.'

Reducing consumption is a much easier task, though, than tackling population growth, he says: 'What many of my colleagues share with me is the view that we would like to see a gradual decline in population, but a rapid decline in consumption habits. We utterly transformed our consumption habits and patterns of economy in the US between 1941 and 1945, and then back again. If you've got the right incentives, you can change patterns of consumption very rapidly.'

So, if you accept the planet is over-populated – a big 'if' for many observers – what are the solutions? 'We have two huge advantages when trying to tackle population growth compared with consumption levels. First, we know what to do about it. If you educate women about their means to control reproduction, the odds are you will see a decline in fertility rates. Second, everyone understands the problem: you can't keep growing the number of people on a finite planet.

'But many economists still want people to consume more to get our economy back, but this will just see more resources destroyed. We also don't have what I'd call "consumption condoms". One of my colleagues once joked that the Government ought to send round a truck to your home the day after you've been on a spending spree and offer to take everything you've bought back to the store. It would be the equivalent of a consumption morning-after pill.'

The seven-billion figure is eye-catching, but behind it lies a complicated demographic reality. For example, population growth in developed nations has largely stagnated. Even in places traditionally associated with rapid population growth, such as Bangladesh, birth rates have fallen considerably over the last generation, yet remain well above the natural replenishment rate of just above two children per woman. The only place where birth rates still remain at pre-industrial-age rates – six or more children per woman – is Sub-Saharan Africa.

Every region requires its own solution, says Ehrlich. 'In the US, where the population has risen by 10% in a decade, largely due to immigration, it is super critical that we tackle the population rise because we are super consumers. But, in general, in the rich countries where population growth has stopped or fallen, we should now be concentrating on reducing per capita consumption levels.'

Ehrlich says that he is far more pessimistic now than he was when he wrote *The Population Bomb*. Increased immigration is an inevitability caused by increasing population and it will, he says, 'become an ever-increasing political nightmare'.

He also laments the lost opportunities: 'The only thing we have done which was beneficial – but possibly fatal in the long run – was the "green revolution". But technological rabbits pulled out of the hat often have very nasty droppings. Frankly, I don't think most people are even remotely aware of what needs to be done to make our world a pleasant place to live in by, say, 2050.'

We've got more than enough land upon which to collectively sustain ourselves, we just need to use it more wisely and fairly

---

James Lovelock, the independent scientist who first proposed the Gaia theory, is another prominent environmental thinker who has prescribed a bleak future for the human species if it continues to grow without restriction. He now advises people to 'enjoy it while you can' because the outlook for future generations is, he believes, so stark.

'We do keep expecting a crash, as Malthus said, but then technology steps in, or something else, and alters the whole game,' he says. 'But it has its limit: it doesn't go to infinity. I expect we'll muddle through for the next 50 years, but sooner or later it will catch up with us.'

Lovelock believes nations such as the UK now resemble a lifeboat: 'In the UK, our population is growing slightly. It's containable. We do grow quite a bit of our food, so we should be OK, provided our climate doesn't change drastically. We could drop our calorie intake without noticing it in health terms. In fact, we'd improve our health like we did in the Second World War.

'But I think we should call a halt to all immigration, or encourage people to go abroad. The average American has about ten times as much land as we do. We're one of the most densely populated places in the world. In some respects, England is one large city. If you want to keep stuffing people in, you'll have to pay the price. I see us as a lifeboat with the person in charge saying: 'We can't take any more, or else we'll all sink.' America, meanwhile, could handle lots more immigration. Not politically, perhaps, but in terms of shared resources and land.'

14 January 2011

THE GUARDIAN

The overpopulation myth

The idea that growing human numbers will destroy the planet is nonsense. But over-consumption will.

By Fred Pearce

Many of today's most-respected thinkers, from Stephen Hawking to David Attenborough, argue that our efforts to fight climate change and other environmental perils will all fail unless we 'do something' about population growth. In *The Universe in a Nutshell*, Hawking declares that, 'in the last 200 years, population growth has become exponential… The world population doubles every 40 years.'

But this is nonsense. For a start, there is no exponential growth. In fact, population growth is slowing. For more than three decades now, the average number of babies being born to women in most of the world has been in decline. Globally, women today have half as many babies as their mothers did, mostly out of choice. They are doing it for their own good, the good of their families, and, if it helps the planet too, then so much the better.

Here are the numbers. 40 years ago, the average woman had between five and six kids. Now she has 2.6. This is getting close to the replacement level which, allowing for girls who don't make it to adulthood, is around 2.3. As I show in my new book, *Peoplequake*, half the world already has a fertility rate below the long-term replacement level. That includes all of Europe, much of

the Caribbean and the Far East from Japan to Vietnam and Thailand, Australia, Canada, Sri Lanka, Turkey, Algeria, Kazakhstan and Tunisia.

It also includes China, where the state decides how many children couples can have. This is brutal and repulsive. But the odd thing is that it may not make much difference any more: Chinese communities around the world have gone the same way without any compulsion – Taiwan, Singapore, and even Hong Kong. When Britain handed Hong Kong back to China in 1997, it had the lowest fertility rate in the world: below one child per woman.

So why is this happening? Demographers used to say that women only started having fewer children when they became educated and the economy got rich, as in Europe. But tell that to the women of Bangladesh, one of the world's poorest nations, where girls are among the least educated in the world, and mostly marry in their mid-teens. They have just three children now, less than half the number their mothers had. India is even lower, at 2.8. Tell that also to the women of Brazil. In this hotbed of Catholicism, women have two children on average – and this is falling. Nothing the priests say can stop it.

Women are doing this because, for the first time in history, they can. Better healthcare and sanitation mean that most babies now live to grow up. It is no longer necessary to have five or six children to ensure the next generation – so they don't.

There are holdouts, of course. In parts of rural Africa, women still have five or more children. But even here they are being rational. Women mostly run the farms, and they need the kids to mind the animals and work in the fields.

Then there is the Middle East, where traditional patriarchy still rules. In remote villages in Yemen, girls as young as 11 are forced into marriage. They still have six babies on average. But even the Middle East is changing. Take Iran. In the past 20 years, Iranian women have gone from having eight children to fewer than two – 1.7 in fact – whatever the mullahs say.

The big story here is that rich or poor, socialist or capitalist, Muslim or Catholic, secular or devout, with or without tough government birth-control policies in place, most countries tell the same tale of a reproductive revolution.

That doesn't mean population growth has ceased. The world's population is still rising by 70 million a year. This

Stop ruining it for everybody else!

CONSUMER AND PROUD OF IT

Facts on satisfying the need for contraception in developing countries

Information from the International Planned Parenthood Federation and the Guttmacher Institute.

Why contraception is critical

⇨ The benefits of contraceptive use are dramatic and far-reaching. They include preventing unintended pregnancies, reducing the number of abortions, and reducing the incidence of deaths and illnesses related to complications of pregnancy and childbirth.

⇨ Contraceptive use enables couples to have the number of children they want and can care for, can reduce the transmission of HIV, helps reduce pressure on scarce natural resources, and can improve educational and employment opportunities for women and their children. These improvements in turn contribute to reducing poverty and spurring economic growth.

⇨ Increased contraceptive use and reduced unmet need for contraception are indicators of progress toward two of the United Nations Millennium Development Goals – reducing maternal mortality and reversing the spread of HIV/AIDS – and contribute directly or indirectly to achieving all eight goals.

⇨ Two trends will likely drive up demand for contraceptives in the future. First, the number of women of reproductive age (15–49) will increase by 10% between 2007 and 2015 and by another 8% between 2015 and 2025. Second, contraceptive needs are expected to rise as increasing numbers of women want to have smaller families. As a result, increased investment in contraceptive services will become even more crucial.

Demand and unmet need for contraception

⇨ Survey data from developing countries, primarily from the Demographic and Health Surveys (DHS), provide information about the demand for and use of contraceptives. A woman is defined as needing contraception if she is married, in a union, or unmarried and sexually active; is able to become pregnant; and does not want to have a child in the next two years or at all. According to the DHS definition, if a woman wanting to avoid pregnancy is using any method of contraception, either modern or traditional, her need is met (or satisfied), and if she is not, she has an 'unmet need' for contraception.

⇨ In Africa, about one in five married women of childbearing age (22%) have an unmet need for

Key demographic indicators, 2011

Even though the Democratic Republic of Congo (DRC) and Italy have almost the same population today, the DRC is projected to more than double its population by 2050. Italy's population, however, is projected to grow by just one million over that same time. The cause of these enormous differences is lifetime births per woman and the share of the population in their childbearing years.

	Congo, Democratic Republic	Italy
Population mid-2011	68 million	61 million
Population 2050 (projected)	149 million	62 million
Percentage of population below age 15	46%	14%
Per cent of population age 65+	3%	20%
Lifetime births per woman	6.1	1.4
Annual births	3,050,000	560,000
Annual deaths	1,140,000	590,000
Infant mortality rate (per 1,000 live births)	111	3.7
Annual infant deaths	340,000	2,000
Gross national income per capita, 2009	$300	$31,870

Source: 2011 World population data sheet, © *Population Reference Bureau*

GUTTMACHER INSTITUTE

contraception. The proportion has changed little since the mid-1990s, when 24% had an unmet need.

⇨ Declines in unmet need among married women have been larger in Asia and Latin America and the Caribbean: from 18% to 13% and 16% to 10%, respectively.

⇨ In some countries in Western, Eastern and Southern Africa, unmet need has declined very little; in a few countries, including Mozambique and Uganda, unmet need has increased.

⇨ Comparatively little is known about the contraceptive needs of unmarried women in developing countries. In Asia and North Africa, for example, estimates of unmet need are not available for this group because unmarried women are either not interviewed or not asked about their reproductive health preferences or behaviours.

⇨ In most countries in Latin America and the Caribbean, 30–50% of sexually active unmarried women aged 15–24 are not using any contraceptive method. In Sub-Saharan Africa, these levels range from 25% to 60%. The levels have gradually declined in the last decade as contraceptive use has increased. However, assuming most of these women do not want to have a child in the near future, these figures represent high levels of unmet need among unmarried women.

Unmet needs among specific groups

⇨ Levels of unmet need for contraception vary greatly among subgroups of women both at the regional level and within countries. Women who are young, uneducated, poor or living in rural areas are generally at high risk of having an unintended pregnancy.

⇨ Among married women, unmet need for contraception is highest among those aged 15–24. Unmet need declines with age in several Latin American, Caribbean and Asian countries, but, in many Sub-Saharan African countries, it is similar among women in all age groups; in a few others, it is highest among women aged 35 and older.

⇨ Historical trends show that educated, urban and financially better-off women have begun to want smaller families and therefore have needed contraceptives earlier than their less-educated and poorer peers. Thus, educated, urban and better-off women may experience unmet need first, when their desire to have fewer children outpaces their access to and use of contraceptives. Eventually, the demand for contraceptives rises among women in poor and rural areas as well, usually leading to an increase in unmet need in these groups.

⇨ Nearly everywhere, unmet need is higher among women living in rural areas than among those in urban areas. In a few countries in Sub-Saharan Africa, however, unmet need is greater among urban women than rural women. These countries are in the early stages of adopting family planning.

⇨ In many countries, unmet need is also higher among less-educated women than more-educated women, and among poor women compared with better-off women. Many Sub-Saharan African countries are an exception, in that levels of unmet need are fairly equal across wealth categories. Some of the largest disparities in unmet need according to wealth can be found in Latin America and the Caribbean and in Asia.

⇨ While unmet need has declined among married women of all educational levels in most of Asia, Latin America and the Caribbean, and North Africa in the past 15–20 years, unmet need rose among uneducated women in some Sub-Saharan African countries. The trend in Sub-Saharan Africa is likely explained by a growing desire to limit or space births that has not yet been matched by an increase in contraceptive use.

Updated November 2010

⇨ Guttmacher Institute, Facts on Satisfying the Need for Contraception in Developing Countries, *In Brief,* New York: Guttmacher Institute, 2010 (http://www.guttmacher.org/pubs/FB-Unmet-Need-Intl.pdf). Accessed 21/11/2011

You promised me that you would have the next baby!

GUTTMACHER INSTITUTE

Chapter 2

MIGRATION TRENDS

Migration

We live in the Age of Migration, with a record 200 million people, or 3% of the world population, now living outside their country of birth.

Migration as such is not new. Studies by palaeoanthropologists suggest that our human ancestors, and other hominids before them, have been migrating since the earliest times for which we have evidence. More recently, many significant migrations have been recorded: to take just one example, that from Europe to North America in the 19th century. The difference today is the scale and continuous nature of movement of people around the world – and the fact that there are no more 'empty continents' for us to occupy.

Widening inequality between high- and low-income countries acts as a strong driver for migration. Migrants hope for a better quality of life by living in a wealthier country, or they may seek to work abroad and send money back to relatives at home. Migration may also be a measure of last resort, in response to deteriorating trade conditions, political persecution, oppression or war. In some instances, migration is due to environmental changes which the people concerned have no control over. However, in other cases, an increase in population to levels that are unsustainable for the country concerned results in a progressive deterioration of living conditions and drives migration. An increase in the number of people that are reliant on finite quantities of food, land, water and other resources invariably reduces the amount available per capita. Competition for these increasingly scarce resources can lead to conflict, with large numbers of people becoming refugees.

Climate change is likely to increase migratory pressures. Many of the regions where agricultural output is predicted to be most adversely affected by changes in temperature or rainfall are already highly populated. One tragic example is the conflict between pastoralists and herders for access to land in Darfur. In Northern Darfur, the almost unprecedented scale of climate change is causing desertification; this has put considerable stress on traditional agriculture and pastoralist livelihoods.

The conflict has displaced 2.7 million people internally. It has also forced 250,000 people to cross the border to Chad, where they now languish in UN refugee camps.

Another predicted result of climate change, a rise in sea levels, is expected to displace many millions. A one-metre rise, for example, would force displacement of 50 million people in 84 developing countries. Combined with other effects of climate change, such as salination of groundwater supply, flooding and climate change could increase the forecast number of 'environmental refugees' to 200 million by 2050.

For destination countries, migrants can reduce labour and skill shortages and contribute to a country's cultural diversity, although large-scale migration can also lead to social divisions and tension. However, even if social integration proceeds well, increased numbers are likely to put pressure on the resources of their adoptive country. Immigration into developed countries may not appear to cause a resource problem in itself, until one considers where the resources come from. The UK, for instance, already imports a large proportion of its food, goods and energy. As worldwide competition for diminishing resources grows, the consequences of the dependence of developed countries on developing countries for their imports will become painfully evident.

Migration in the UK

The UK's population is already more than 60 million, making it one of the most densely populated countries in Europe and therefore among those most dependent on imports in order to provide for its citizens. Moreover, its population is currently projected to increase to more than 70 million by 2050. Providing for this number of people will require a massive increase in investment in services and infrastructure, as well as increasing the demand for food, energy and many other resources.

The projected increase in numbers is partly the result of people living longer, but at least half of it is expected to be caused by continued net inward migration. We should, of course, continue to support the right to political asylum, but those seeking political asylum currently only represent a small proportion of the total. Figures suggest that approximately 25% of migrants arrive for work-related reasons, around 25% in order to accompany or join a partner, around 25% for study,

and the remainder for other reasons, including those as yet unemployed who are looking for work.

It has often been stated that the economy benefits from the presence of immigrant workers, to fill both low-paid unskilled jobs and some highly skilled ones. But the extent to which this is true is uncertain and it has been disputed by a House of Lords study. What is clear is that the country simply cannot support an ever-

increasing number of people, irrespective of whether this is caused by immigration exceeding emigration or births exceeding deaths.

⇨ The above information is reprinted with kind permission from Population Matters. Visit www.populationmatters.org for more information.

© Population Matters

Migration: facts and figures

Global estimates and trends.

⇨ 214 million – estimated number of international migrants worldwide.

↳ The total number of international migrants has increased over the last ten years from an estimated 150 million in 2000 to 214 million persons today.

⇨ 3.1% – percentage of the world's population who are migrants.

↳ In other words, one of out of every 33 persons in the world today is a migrant (whereas in 2000 one out of every 35 persons was a migrant).

↳ The percentage of migrants has remained relatively stable as a share of the total population, increasing by only 0.2 per cent (from 2.9 to 3.1 per cent), over the last decade.

↳ However, the percentage of migrants varies greatly from country to country. Countries with a high percentage of migrants include Qatar (87 per cent), United Arab Emirates (70 per cent), Jordan (46 per cent), Singapore (41 per cent) and Saudi Arabia (28 per cent).

↳ Countries with a low percentage of migrants include South Africa (3.7 per cent), Slovakia (2.4 per cent), Turkey (1.9 per cent), Japan (1.7 per cent), Nigeria (0.7 per cent), Romania (0.6 per cent), India (0.4 per cent) and Indonesia (0.1 per cent).

⇨ Migrants would constitute the fifth most populous country in the world.

↳ Migration is now more widely distributed across more countries. Today the top ten countries of destination receive a smaller share of all migrants than in 2000.

⇨ 49% – percentage of migrants worldwide who are women.

⇨ $440 billion – estimated remittances sent by migrants in 2010.

↳ Remittances have increased exponentially: up from US$132 billion in 2000 to an estimated US$440 billion in 2010, even with a slight decline due to the current economic crisis.

↳ The actual amount, including unrecorded flows through formal and informal channels, is believed to be significantly larger.

↳ In 2010, the top recipient countries of recorded remittances were India, China, Mexico, the Philippines and France.

↳ Rich countries are the main source of remittances. The United States is by far the largest, with US$48.3 billion in recorded outward flows in 2009. Saudi Arabia ranks as the second largest, followed by Switzerland and Russia.

⇨ US$325 billion – estimated remittances sent by migrants to developing countries in 2010.

⇨ 27.5 million – internally displaced persons in the world in 2010.

↳ IDP numbers have grown from 21 million in 2000 to 27.5 million at the end of 2010.

⇨ 15.4 million – number of refugees in the world today.

↳ Based on data from the UN High Commissioner for Refugees, the number of refugees stood at 15.4 million in 2010 compared to 15.9 million in 2000 – a decline of around 500,000. However, due to a change in classification and estimation methodology in a number of countries, figures as from 2007 are not fully comparable with pre-2007 figures.

↳ The proportion of refugees in migrant stocks has fallen from 8.8 per cent in 2000 to 7.6 per cent in 2010.

⇨ The above information was compiled by and reprinted with kind permission from the International Organization for Migration. For a complete list of sources, please visit www.iom.int.

© The International Organization for Migration

POPULATION MATTERS / THE INTERNATIONAL ORGANIZATION FOR MIGRATION

Targeting uncertainty?
EU migration in the UK

Information from the Migration Observatory.

Today's migration data release from the ONS makes the Government's efforts to reduce net migration from 239,000 in 2010 (the number reported today) to the tens of thousands by 2015 more difficult than ever. Today's figures show the highest annual level of net migration since 2004 and a 21% increase from 2009.

One of the key difficulties and uncertainties that the Government faces in hitting its overall net migration target is that there are several factors that the UK cannot control – with perhaps the most obvious being immigration and emigration of British and other EU citizens. Today's evidence of a steep rise in net migration from Eastern Europe is testament to the challenges this causes for the Government and raises the question of whether Government policies to cut net migration from outside the EU may be stimulating a demand for more EU workers.

Today's figures show the highest annual level of net migration since 2004 and a 21% increase from 2009

It is worth remembering what is actually meant by 'net migration'. The term refers to the balance between migrants entering a country (immigration) and people leaving a country (emigration). 'Positive' net migration occurs when more people arrive than leave and 'negative' net migration occurs when the opposite happens.

The impact of total EU migration (this includes immigration and emigration of British people) on total net migration in the UK has – until recently – been very small. This is because positive net migration of non-British EU nationals has been almost completely offset by negative net migration of British citizens.

In 2009 there was positive EU net migration of around 14,000 (which is comprised of −44,000 for British and 58,000 for non-British EU citizens). Since 2004 annual net EU migration has fluctuated between a high point of 30,000 (2007) and a low point of −24,000 (2008). During that five-year period from 2004–2009 there was negative net EU migration of −12,000 (the difference between −547,000 British net migration and +535,000 other EU net migration).

But there is no reason to think that there is some form of natural balance between British and other EU net migration that will be maintained indefinitely. We do not yet have final data for 2010 but today's provisional figures from the ONS – based on data from the International Passenger Survey – suggest that British net migration remains negative but the difference between British emigration and immigration is smaller than the 2004–2009 average. At the same time, the data suggest a significant increase in net migration of 'A8' nationals – citizens of the eight East European countries that joined the EU in May 2004 – from 5,000 in 2009 to 39,000 in 2010.

Looking at the employment of working-age A8 migrants in the UK, for which we have more recent data, we can see that the number grew from around 52,000 in the first quarter of 2004 to 504,000 in the third quarter of 2008, slightly declined to a level that fluctuated between 469,000 and 500,000 in 2008 and 2009 (presumably due to the recession), but has been growing again since early 2010 and in the second quarter of 2011 was at its highest level ever: 651,000.

The UK clearly remains an attractive destination for migrants from A8 countries. Despite all EU member states having had to open their labour markets to A8 workers, the factors that created the initial pull for A8 workers to the UK are still in place – there is a demand for their labour, wages are still much higher than Poland or other A8 nations and there are now well-established A8 communities and networks here to help new and returning EU migrants find a job and negotiate the complexities of life in a new country.

This adds up to the likelihood that the UK's population of Eastern Europeans will continue to increase for some time, as there are no signs on the horizon that the overall trend of positive A8 net migration to the UK will end soon.

The small reduction in 2008 and 2009 does suggest that if the UK goes into recession again there may be another temporary fall in the number of A8 migrants in the workforce, but it is also worth considering that, as the Government continues to focus on reducing non-EU net migration, employers may turn increasingly to EU migrants to fill positions. In a recent survey by the Chartered Institute of Personnel and Development, 34 per cent of employers said they intend to respond to the Government's new policies by recruiting more EU migrants whereas only 23 per cent said they intend to respond by increasing the skills of their current workforce.

Any sustained increase in net migration of A8 workers makes it substantially harder for the Government to reduce overall net migration to the tens of thousands.

The fundamental problem the Government faces is that its target of reducing net migration to the 'tens of thousands' contains elements over which the Government has varying levels of influence. When it comes to migration of non-EU nationals the Government has considerable, although variable, degrees of control – with more control over workers and students than over family members or asylum seekers. But the Government cannot control the immigration and emigration of British and other EU nationals.

This means that, regardless of the reductions in non-EU net migration achieved by Government policy, there will always be fundamental uncertainty about whether any overall net migration target will be hit. This fundamental uncertainty cannot be reduced unless the target is reformulated to apply to non-EU migration only.

⇨ The above information is reprinted with kind permission from the Migration Observatory. Visit www.migrationobservatory.ox.ac.uk for more information.

© Migration Observatory

Immigration cap fails to reduce numbers coming to UK

The Government wants immigration drastically reduced.

By Ian Dunt

The immigration cap appears to have had no effect on the number of people coming to the UK, with a 20% rise over the last year.

Official figures showed net immigration jumped to 239,000, although a reduction in the number of Brits leaving the country contributed to the figures.

'These figures reveal the gulf between the Government's rhetoric on immigration, and the reality we see in the official figures,' said Shabana Mahmood, shadow Home Office minister.

'The Government is not being honest with the British public. They have shown a keen interest in hyperbole around immigration, doing everything they can to make it a party-political issue, but they are busy further eroding trust in government's ability to manage it.'

The Government intends to cut annual net immigration down to 'the tens of thousands' by 2015 and tried to achieve this by limiting skilled workers from outside the EU.

This appears to have had little effect, with employers mostly taking the workers needed from inside the EU and immigration to the UK remaining fairly steady.

Emigration, however, has fallen – down over 20% since 2008.

A sluggish world economy seems to have discouraged Brits from leaving to find work elsewhere.

Immigration from Eastern Europe was up from 52,000 to 71,000, in a sign that employers were forced to find skilled workers from inside the EU to fill job vacancies.

Meanwhile, the number of Eastern Europeans emigrating back home was down from 47,000 to 31,000.

While many Eastern Europeans returned to their home countries when the recession first hit Britain, that trend appears to have calmed down.

The Government's focus on student migration also appears to have had little effect, with a reduction of just one per cent since last year.

25 August 2011

⇨ The above information is reprinted with kind permission from Politics.co.uk. Visit www.politics.co.uk for more information.

© Politics.co.uk

MIGRATION OBSERVATORY / POLITICS.CO.UK

Europeans think the number of immigrants allowed into their country should be dictated by the national government, not the European Union. The British Government agrees: Theresa May last year said that the plans for a common asylum system represented an unacceptable loss of sovereignty.

But the desire for national control is not only about practical impacts on resources – it also relates to a sense of fairness, and, more precisely, the suspicion seen in many countries that they are taking more than their fair share of the burden. For example, in Britain six in ten think we take proportionally more asylum seekers than other countries – despite the fact that we rank mid-table in Europe on asylum applications. To go back to Barroso's quote, misperceptions are important too.

The European Council's recent ruling to allow for the reintroduction of internal border controls within the Schengen area (which covers much of Europe, but excludes Britain) in 'exceptional' circumstances is evidence of the anxiety in some continental European states.

Our forthcoming report on attitudes to the Schengen Agreement also provides a fascinating insight into how deep concerns run in Britain. From the nine countries included in the study, the one most likely to support the reintroduction of border controls was Britain – even though we've never given ours up. Not only do we want greater control over who visits Britain, we're not keen on freedom of movement between other countries.

The political accountability of governments to their populations means Britain and every other EU state does not want to look like they're carrying the 'burden' for the rest of Europe, even where this is based on a misreading of the facts. A common European approach is particularly politically toxic in Britain, given two-thirds distrust the EU itself, higher than any other European country.

Perceptions are key, and we've seen how pro-immigration arguments over the last few years have at best left the public unmoved, and at worst hardened views by seeming so out of touch. It will be an even harder task to convince people this is an issue that can be solved through greater international cooperation, not less.

Bobby Duffy is managing director of Ipsos MORI's Social Research Institute and director of the global Ipsos Social Research Institute.

August 2011

⇨ The above information is reprinted with kind permission from Ipsos MORI. Visit www.ipsos-mori.com for more information.

© *Ipsos MORI*

Immigration 'could cost social housing £25 billion'

A pressure group has claimed that housing new immigrants in social homes will cost the taxpayer around £1 billion a year for 25 years.

MigrationWatch UK published a study today which it says shows that, if government projections for immigration and housing need in England stay the same, 45 extra social homes would have to be built each day.

The group is basing its research on the Government's 25-year projection of household numbers from 2008 to 2033.

It is also assuming immigration figures stay on course.

The group argues that 20 per cent of migrant households currently live in social housing and say that 415,000 extra social homes will be needed in total.

MigrationWatch UK say that with average funding of around £60,000 per each social housing unit, the final bill would be around £25 billion.

Sir Andrew Green, chairman of MigrationWatch UK, said: 'The impact of immigration on the availability of social housing for British people has been airbrushed out for too long.

MigrationWatch UK say that with average funding of around £60,000 per each social housing unit, the final bill would be around £25 billion

'Either the Government must cut immigration very substantially as they have promised or they must invest very large sums in the construction of extra social housing.'

The group say that on average, 17 per cent of UK-born people currently live in social housing while the figure rises to 80 per cent of Somali people.

According to the figures, Polish people are the least likely to be staying in social housing at just eight per cent of the population.

17 August 2011

⇨ The above information is reprinted with kind permission from Inside Housing. Visit www. insidehousing.co.uk for more information.

© *Inside Housing*

MigrationWatch claims migrants are driving social housing demand

MigrationWatch has published a new claim – dutifully reported by the Daily Express and The Star – that meeting the social housing needs of new immigrants will cost the tax payer £1 billion a year for the next 25 years. However, as John Perry points out, grants for new social housing will total only £4.5 billion for the four years 2011–2015. It is absurd to say that social housing for migrants will cost the taxpayer £1 billion per year as this would be almost the total budget.

By John Perry

MigrationWatch has published a new claim that meeting the social housing needs of new immigrants will cost the tax payer £1 billion a year for the next 25 years. It bases its assessment on the fact that migration is currently expected to lead to the formation of 83,000 new households each year, out of a projected total of 232,000 new households.

These are official figures, but they need to be treated with great caution: population projections are revised regularly and do not take account of the economic situation, which might well lead to a fall in net migration over the next few years.

While the 83,000 households (if the projection is correct) would add to housing demand, so would the 149,000 households due to form from natural population growth. The link between this overall demand and the number of homes that are built is purely theoretical: many of these households will share, many won't qualify for social housing for many years, or be able to afford to buy. In any event, for many years now the number of new houses built has not kept pace with household formation.

The fact is that the Government currently plans to build 150,000 social homes over the next five years and the budgets to do that are already fixed. Much of the money has to come from social landlords' own resources, which means rents will go up. Grants for new social housing will total only £4.5 billion for the four years 2011–2015. It is absurd to say that social housing for migrants will cost the taxpayer £1 billion per year as this would be almost the total budget.

Few, if any, new migrants will qualify to get these homes: the percentage of new social housing lettings going to foreign nationals in any one year is only 7%, and the vast majority of these are likely to be people who have lived in the UK for many years, and have had time to get settled immigration status, to have families and to qualify through waiting lists. As a new briefing from Oxford's Migration Observatory points out, 75% of newly-arrived migrants go into the private rented sector.

The MigrationWatch research paper also tries to link social housing and migration by putting the growth in waiting lists and in net migration on the same graph.

The percentage of new social housing lettings going to foreign nationals in any one year is only 7%

This compares chalk and cheese: only a very small percentage of the new migrants shown would have been eligible to go on waiting lists, and an even smaller proportion would have actually put their names down, for a variety of reasons. An important one is that much of the growth shown is from the new EU countries, most of whose nationals did not initially qualify for social housing anyway.

22 August 2011

⇨ The above information is reprinted with kind permission from Migrants' Rights Network. Visit www.migrantsrights.org.uk for more information.

© *Migrants' Rights Network*

It looks as though a caravan or a tent is the only option?

MIGRANTS' RIGHTS NETWORK

International brain drain: workers looking overseas for a better job in some key markets

⇨ **One in four willing to move countries to find a better job.**

⇨ **One in four looking to leave their employer within 12 months.**

Countries still reeling from the global recession could be set to become employment 'ghost towns' as more than a quarter of workers say they are willing to move overseas to find a better job – according to *GfK International Employee Survey*, a new international report from GfK Custom Research.

The question was asked in 17 of the 29 countries covered by the major international study and found that more than a quarter of the workforce questioned (27 per cent) is willing to move to another country to find better employment.

And it is the young, qualified employees who are most likely to feel this workplace wanderlust: two-fifths (41 per cent) of workers aged 18–29 agreed they are willing to move countries to find a better job, while that figure is one in three for degree holders (32 per cent) and nearly one in four for PhD holders (37 per cent). This is compared to just a fifth of employees educated to secondary-school level (22 per cent).

Dr Ingrid Feinstein at GfK Switzerland comments, 'Our findings indicate a risk of "brain drain" in the coming year, posing significant problems for companies and countries looking to recover from the downturn. Both blue collar and white collar workers show a quarter of their number willing to look overseas for work, and that figure rises for the higher-educated workers. Crucially, a third of people in Research and Development roles are also willing to look overseas – the very roles that many countries identify as key to recovery.'

Latin America is hardest hit

Unsurprisingly, the findings show that Central and South America look set to be the hardest hit of the markets covered. Nearly six in ten Mexican employees (57 per cent), half of Colombia's workforce (52 per cent) and two-fifths of staff in Brazil and Peru (41 and 38 per cent, respectively) are ready to look across borders for better careers.

> *More than a quarter of the workforce questioned (27 per cent) is willing to move to another country to find better employment*

But the trend is far from limited to developing markets. Other markets coming in at the top of the 17 countries asked about willingness to move countries to find a better job include: Turkey in third place with 46 per cent, Hungary in seventh place (33 per cent), followed by Russia (29 per cent) and – coming in with ninth equal – Portugal and the UK with 27 per cent each.

Even the US and Canada – countries traditionally stereotyped for their relative disinterest in living abroad – face a fifth of their workers saying that they are ready to move countries to find a better job, at 21 per cent and 20 per cent, respectively.

As well as countries needing to guard against brain drain across borders, there is a warning for companies too, with more than one in four workers intending to leave their employers within 12 months.

Approval of governments on integrating immigrants, by country

Country	percentage
Canada	51%
United Kingdom	29%
United States	34%
France	31%
Germany	38%
Spain	43%
Italy	26%
Netherlands	19%

Source: Transatlantic Trends: Immigration, © German Marshall Fund of the United States

GFK GROUP

Of those, one in three is already actively looking for a new job (35 per cent) and one in five (18 per cent) looking to move in the next six months. Just eight per cent of employees are looking to wait until the economy is more secure.

As well as countries needing to guard against brain drain across borders, there is a warning for companies too, with more than one in four workers intending to leave their employers within 12 months

The situation looks particularly worrying for Colombia and the USA, where around half (55 per cent and 47 per cent, respectively) of their workers are actively looking to move jobs. At the other end of the scale, Brazil and Belgium face a far more stable retention environment, with only 15 per cent of workers actively looking to change employers.

Today's globalised and fluid labour market

Explaining the figures, Dr Feinstein continued: 'The findings highlight just how globalised and fluid the labour market has become in many countries.

'The truth remains that, for many employees, moving country is no more daunting than moving company. Companies looking to recruit, engage and retain the best staff need to compete, not just with rivals in their own nations and markets, but from right around the world.

'The research also reveals that employees in multinational organisations are those most likely to look elsewhere. This suggests that allowing employees to work overseas is not just a perk but a valuable retention tool.'

About the survey

The *GfK International Employee Engagement Survey* was conducted by international research firm the GfK Custom Research. It includes the opinions of 30,556 working adults in 29 countries who were interviewed between 8 February and 4 April 2011 using online, telephone or in-person interviewing techniques appropriate to the country.

Data were weighted to represent the demographic composition (industry, gender and age) of each country. To produce global statistics that combine countries, the data for each country was also weighted by GDP (PPP).

The questionnaire was developed by an international team of employee engagement experts, with input from experts in each of the 29 countries.

Countries surveyed were: Argentina, Austria, Belgium, Brazil, Bulgaria, Canada, Colombia, Czech Republic, France, Germany, Hungary, Israel, Macedonia, Mexico, the Netherlands, Peru, Philippines, Poland, Portugal, Romania, Russia, Serbia, Slovakia, Sweden, Switzerland, Turkey, UK, Ukraine, USA.

22 June 2011

⇨ The above information is reprinted with kind permission from the GfK Group. Visit www.gfk.com for more information.

What is forced migration?

Information from Forced Migration, University of Oxford.

FMO has adopted the definition of 'forced migration' promoted by the International Association for the Study of Forced Migration (IASFM), which describes it as: 'A general term that refers to the movements of refugees and internally displaced people (those displaced by conflicts) as well as people displaced by natural or environmental disasters, chemical or nuclear disasters, famine, or development projects.' FMO views forced migration as a complex, wide-ranging and pervasive set of phenomena. The study of forced migration is multidisciplinary, international and multisectoral, incorporating academic, practitioner, agency and local perspectives. FMO focuses on three separate, although sometimes simultaneous and inter-related, types of forced migration. These three types are categorised according to their causal factors: conflict, development policies and projects, and disasters.

These three categories of forced migration are often studied by different academic communities; the causes are addressed by different groups of policy-makers, donors and agencies; and the consequences addressed by different governmental, inter-governmental and non-governmental agencies, donors and organisations. FMO attempts to bring together in one place these various groups, approaches and experiences of all forms of forced migration.

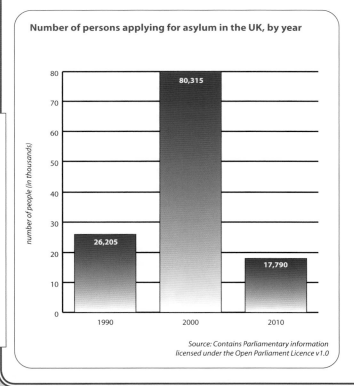

Number of persons applying for asylum in the UK, by year

number of people (in thousands)

- 1990: 26,205
- 2000: 80,315
- 2010: 17,790

Source: Contains Parliamentary information licensed under the Open Parliament Licence v1.0

Types of forced migration

Conflict-induced displacement

People who are forced to flee their homes for one or more of the following reasons and where the state authorities are unable or unwilling to protect them: armed conflict including civil war; generalised violence; and persecution on the grounds of nationality, race, religion, political opinion or social group.

A large proportion of these displaced people will flee across international borders in search of refuge. Some of them may seek asylum under international law, whereas others may prefer to remain anonymous, perhaps fearing that they may not be granted asylum and will be returned to the country from whence they fled. Since the end of the Cold War, there has been an escalation in the number of armed conflicts around the world. Many of these more recent conflicts have been internal conflicts based on national, ethnic or religious separatist struggles. There has been a large increase in the number of refugees during this period as displacement has increasingly become a strategic tactic often used by all sides in the conflict. Since the end of the Cold War there has also been an even more dramatic increase in the number of internally displaced persons (IDPs), who currently far outnumber the world's refugee population. At the end of 2004, there were some 11.5 million refugees and asylum seekers and a further 21 million IDPs worldwide.

The most important international organisation with responsibility for refugees is the United Nations High Commissioner for Refugees (UNHCR). Under the 1951 UN Refugee Convention, UNHCR is mandated to provide protection and assistance to refugees. However, one group of refugees do not come under the mandate of UNHCR. These are Palestinian refugees in the Middle East, who come under the mandate of the United Nations Relief and Works Agency for Palestine Refugees in the Near East (UNRWA).

Development-induced displacement

These are people who are compelled to move as a result of policies and projects implemented to supposedly enhance 'development'. Examples of this include large-scale infrastructure projects such as dams, roads, ports, airports; urban clearance initiatives; mining and deforestation; and the introduction of conservation parks/reserves and biosphere projects.

Affected people usually remain within the borders

of their home country. Although some are resettled, evidence clearly shows that very few of them are adequately compensated. While there are guidelines on restoration for affected populations produced by some major donors to these types of projects, such as the World Bank, there continues to be inadequate access to compensation. This tends to be the responsibility of host governments, and interventions from outside are often deemed inappropriate.

This is undoubtedly a causal factor in displacement more often than armed conflict, although it often takes place with little recognition, support or assistance from outside the affected population. It disproportionately affects indigenous and ethnic minorities, and the urban or rural poor. It has been estimated that during the 1990s, some 90 to 100 million people around the world were displaced as a result of infrastructural development projects. It has also been reported that, on average, ten million people a year are displaced by dam projects alone.

Disaster-induced displacement

This category includes people displaced as a result of natural disasters (floods, volcanoes, landslides, earthquakes), environmental change (deforestation, desertification, land degradation, global warming) and human-made disasters (industrial accidents, radioactivity). Clearly, there is a good deal of overlap between these different types of disaster-induced displacement. For example, the impact of floods and landslides can be greatly exacerbated by deforestation and agricultural activities.

Estimating trends and global figures on people displaced by disaster is even more disputed and problematic than for the other two categories. But there are certainly many millions of people displaced by disasters every year. Several international organisations provide assistance to those affected by disasters, including the International Federation of the Red Cross and Red Crescent Societies, and the World Food Programme. Many non-governmental organisations (international and local) also provide assistance to affected people.
16 September 2011

⇨ The above information is reprinted with kind permission from Forced Migration Online. Visit www.forcedmigration.org/about/whatisfm to view the original of this article.

© Forced Migration Online

Other websites you may find useful

Forced Migration Online (FMO) online library
www.forcedmigration.org/digital-library

Refugee Studies Centre (RSC) website
www.rsc.ox.ac.uk/

Forced Migration Review (FMR) website
www.fmreview.org

FORCED MIGRATION ONLINE

Migration due to climate change demands attention

Governments in Asia and the Pacific need to prepare for a large increase in climate-induced migration in the coming years, says a forthcoming report by the Asian Development Bank (ADB).

Typhoons, cyclones, floods and drought are forcing more and more people to migrate. In the past year alone, extreme weather in Malaysia, Pakistan, the People's Republic of China, the Philippines and Sri Lanka has caused temporary or longer-term dislocation of millions. This process is set to accelerate in coming decades as climate change leads to more extreme weather.

'No international cooperation mechanism has been set up to manage these migration flows, and protection and assistance schemes remain inadequate, poorly coordinated, and scattered,' the report states. 'National governments and the international community must urgently address this issue in a proactive manner.'

On the positive side, the report says that if properly managed, climate-induced migration could actually facilitate human adaptation, creating new opportunities for dislocated populations in less vulnerable environments.

The ADB project, *Policy Options to Support Climate-induced Migration*, is the first international initiative that aims to generate policy and financing recommendations to address climate-induced migration in Asia and the Pacific.

7 February 2011

⇨ The above information is reprinted with kind permission from the Asian Development Bank. Visit www.adb.org for more information.

© Asian Development Bank

These hotspots of climate-induced migration face pressure from swelling populations as rural people seek new lives in cities.

ADB expects to issue the report, *Climate Change and Migration in Asia and the Pacific*, in early March as part of a broader ADB project aimed at increasing awareness of, and enhancing regional preparedness for, migration driven by changing weather patterns.

The report highlights specific risks confronting climate change 'hotspots', including megacities in coastal areas of Asia. These hotspots of climate-induced migration face pressure from swelling populations as rural people seek new lives in cities. The problem is compounded by greater dislocation of people caused by flooding and tropical storms.

'Climate-induced migration will affect poor and vulnerable people more than others,' said Bart W. Édes, Director of ADB's Poverty Reduction, Gender, and Social Development Division. 'In many places, those least capable of coping with severe weather and environmental degradation will be compelled to move with few assets to an uncertain future. Those who stay in their communities will struggle to maintain livelihoods in risk-prone settings at the mercy of nature's whims.'

"I'm a "PEOPLE-OF-THE-WORLD WILL-PULL-TOGETHER AND-FIGHT-CLIMATE-CHANGE" SCEPTIC...."

ASIAN DEVELOPMENT BANK

Climate refugee 'crisis' will not result in mass migration – new research

Researchers dismiss 'alarmist predictions' about hundreds of millions of people being forced to migrate across international borders because of climate change.

Climate change is more likely to lead to local and regional migration as people's livelihoods are lost through drought, flooding or other types of environmental degradation. Research by the International Institute for Environment and Development (IIED) in Africa and South America found most migrants were likely to move to other rural areas or local towns on a temporary basis.

Seasonal movement is historically common with, for example, pastoralists in East Africa having long-developed strategies to cope with unpredictable environments. In Sub-Saharan Africa, the study found, many women migrate to towns during dry seasons to work as cleaners and street traders. While in the Bolivian Andes, women are already moving for three to six months of the year to take llamas to pasture.

A number of non-governmental organisations (NGOs) have predicted as many as one billion people could have been forced to relocate by 2050 because of the effects of climate change. However, the IIED findings back up other research that suggests relocation is likely to be local with people whose livelihoods are most sensitive to the environment also tending to be the ones who do not have the means to move very far.

The study says farmers should be helped to diversify their incomes to provide a 'safety net' against environmental degradation. But governments often view migrants as a problem and provide little support, the study found. As a result, when people have relocated they are often returning back to their original homes due to frustration with the lack of help in adapting to a new climate and different agricultural practices.

'Policymakers need to redefine migration and see it as a valuable adaptive response to environmental risks and not as a problem that needs to be tackled,' said study author Dr Cecilia Tacoli, who said she was worried alarmist predictions would backfire and result in policies that marginalise the poorest and most vulnerable groups.

Farmers should be helped to diversify their incomes to provide a 'safety net' against environmental degradation

The Environmental Justice Foundation (EJF) says it still wants climate refugees to be given legal protection by the UN and international community.

'Whilst migration can be a positive adaptation strategy to environmental change, we must not lose sight of the fact that some people are being forcibly displaced. Climate change is putting vulnerable people into more precarious situations,' said EJF executive director Steve Trent. 'This is exactly what we found in Bangladesh, where families told us how their homes had been torn down overnight by cyclones and that their land remains inundated by floodwater. They did not have a choice, they had to move without warning or an opportunity to prepare or plan where to go.'

'Currently there are no legal provisions for people displaced as a result of climate change. That is why EJF is calling for a new international instrument for their recognition and protection,' he added.

4 February 2011

⇨ The above information is reprinted with kind permission from *The Ecologist*. Visit www.theecologist. org for more information.

© *The Ecologist*

That settles it. This year we're planting rice!

THE ECOLOGIST

KEY FACTS

➪ Even though the world population growth rate has slowed from 2.1 per cent per year in the late 1960s to 1.2 per cent today, the size of the world's population has continued to increase – from five billion in 1987 to six billion in 1999, and to seven billion in 2011. (page 1)

➪ It is fundamental to remember that all population projections, whether performed by a national statistical office, the United Nations, or the US Census Bureau, are based on assumptions. (page 2)

➪ Demographers point to a phenomenon called the 'demographic transition', whereby fertility tends to decline as socio-economic development progresses. (page 3)

➪ Since 1950 the richest fifth of humanity has doubled its consumption of energy, meat, timber, steel and copper per person and quadrupled its car ownership, while the poorest fifth of humanity has increased its general consumption hardly at all. (page 5)

➪ Fertility, mortality, migration, economic development, poverty and governance are the main drivers of population growth. (page 9)

➪ A survey commissioned by Population Matters found that over four out of five (84%) thought the world population was too high, with over half (53%) thinking it was much too high. (page 10)

➪ In Africa, about one in five married women of childbearing age (22%) have an unmet need for contraception. (page 16)

➪ Beijing is considering whether to adopt a two-child policy within the next five years, ending the three-decade-old one-child rule, Chinese media have reported. (page 18)

➪ We live in the Age of Migration, with a record 200 million people, or 3% of the world population, now living outside their country of birth. (page 20)

➪ The percentage of migrants varies greatly from country to country. Countries with a high percentage of migrants include Qatar (87 per cent), United Arab Emirates (70 per cent), Jordan (46 per cent), Singapore (41 per cent), and Saudi Arabia (28 per cent). (page 21)

➪ The *Transatlantic Trends* study showed that overestimation of immigrant numbers rose in 2010 in the United States, with respondents believing 39% of the population was born abroad, up from 35% in 2009. The real figure is less than 14%. (page 23)

➪ One of the key difficulties and uncertainties that the Government faces in hitting its overall net migration target is that there are several factors that the UK cannot control – with perhaps the most obvious being immigration and emigration of British and other EU citizens. (Page 24)

➪ The immigration cap appears to have had no effect on the number of people coming to the UK, with a 20% rise over the last year. (page 25)

➪ Seven in ten (71%) Britons say there are too many immigrants in the country and just a quarter (27%) believe immigration is good for the economy according to new research from Ipsos MORI. (page 27)

➪ 76% of Britons believe immigration has placed too much pressure on public services. (page 27)

➪ Research shows that labour migrants leave quickly if they are out of work. (page 34)

➪ Developing-world mothers, too poor to feed their families, are increasingly finding work abroad and sending the fruits of their labour to the children they will not raise. (page 35)

➪ Typhoons, cyclones, floods and drought are forcing more and more people to migrate. In the past year alone, extreme weather in Malaysia, Pakistan, the People's Republic of China, the Philippines and Sri Lanka has caused temporary or longer-term dislocation of millions. (page 38)

Ageing population

A population whose average age is rising. This can be caused by increased life expectancy, for example following significant medical advances, or by falling birth rates, for example due to the introduction of contraception. However, the higher the proportion of older people within a population, the lower the birth rate will become due to there being fewer people of childbearing age.

Asylum seeker

Someone who has fled their country because they personally are at risk of political violence or persecution, and seek the protection of another state.

Birth rate

The number of live births within a population over a given period of time, often expressed as the number of births per 1,000 of the population.

Brain drain

'Brain drain' is a term which refers to the emigration of highly-skilled people from within a population. The resulting lack of skilled workers can have significant economic and social implications for a country or region.

Death rate

The number of deaths within a population over a given period of time, often expressed as number of deaths per 1,000 of the population.

Demographics

Statistical characteristics of a population: for example, age, race or employment status.

Emigration

Leaving one's native country to live in another state. People emigrate for many reasons, but most often with the aim of seeking out better living and working conditions.

Immigrant

A person living in a country to which they are not native. There are many social and cultural issues associated with immigration, particularly the integration of immigrants into the native population.

Infant mortality rate

The number of infant deaths (infants are usually defined as one year old or younger) per 1,000 live births of the population.

Migration

To migrate is to move from one's home country and settle in another.

Population growth

An increase in the number of people who inhabit a specific region. This is caused by a higher birth rate and net immigration than the death rate and net emigration. Since the start of the 20th century the rate of global population growth has increased drastically, growing from just 1.6 billion at the turn of the 20th century to seven billion today.

Refugee

A person who has left their native country in order to escape war, persecution or natural disaster. Refugee status is granted in line with the *United Nations Convention Relating to the Status of Refugees*, which defines which persons are eligible for asylum and which are not: for example, war criminals.

Remittances

Money sent by immigrants back to their home country, often through provisions for their family.

Sustainable population

A population which has enough natural resources within its environment to thrive, but uses them in a manner which allows for them to be constantly renewed and replaced, thereby ensuring that resources will be available to future generations.

ACKNOWLEDGEMENTS

The publisher is grateful for permission to reproduce the following material.

While every care has been taken to trace and acknowledge copyright, the publisher tenders its apology for any accidental infringement or where copyright has proved untraceable. The publisher would be pleased to come to a suitable arrangement in any such case with the rightful owner.

Chapter One: Population Pressure

The world at seven billion, © Population Reference Bureau, *Population growth*, © Politics.co.uk, *Population and human development: the key connections*, © People and Planet, *Population facts*, © United Nations, *Population: assessment of global megatrends*, © European Environment Agency, *Most think UK population 'too high'*, © Population Matters, *The population explosion*, © Guardian News and Media Limited, *The overpopulation myth*, © Prospect Magazine, *Population bomb or consumption explosion?*, © New Economics Foundation, *Facts on satisfying the need for contraception in developing countries*, © Guttmacher Institute, *China considers relaxing one-child policy*, © Guardian News and Media Limited, *Population goals*, © Population Matters.

Chapter Two: Migration Trends

Migration, © Population Matters, *Migration: facts and figures*, © The International Organization for Migration, *Transatlantic trends: immigration*, © German Marshall Fund of the United States, *Targeting uncertainty? EU migration in the UK*, © Migration Observatory, *Immigration cap fails to reduce numbers coming to UK*, © Politics.co.uk, *Britain's animosity to immigration should be addressed, not exploited*, © Wessex Scene, *Too many immigrants?*, © Ipsos MORI, *Immigration 'could cost social housing £25 billion'*, © Inside Housing,

MigrationWatch claims migrants are driving social housing demand, © Migrants' Rights Network, *David Cameron launches immigration crackdown*, © Guardian News and Media Limited, *Recession causes drop in EU immigration: OECD*, © EurActiv.com, *International brain drain: workers looking overseas for a better job in some key markets*, © GfK Group, *Jobless immigrants prefer to leave*, © Economic and Social Research Council, *Mothers and money*, © Global Envision, *What is forced migration?*, © Forced Migration Online, *Migration due to climate demands attention*, © Asian Development Bank, *Climate refugee 'crisis' will not result in mass migration – new research*, © The Ecologist.

Illustrations

Pages 1, 19, 24, 38: Simon Kneebone; pages 13, 23, 34, 39: Angelo Madrid; pages 13, 23, 34, 37: Don Hatcher; pages 10, 14: Bev Aisbett.

Cover photography

Left: © Nate Brelsford. Centre: © Robin Utracik, Northern Studios. Right: © Kriss Szkurlatowski.

Additional acknowledgements

Editorial by Carolyn Kirby on behalf of Independence.

With thanks to the Independence team: Mary Chapman, Sandra Dennis and Jan Sunderland.

Lisa Firth
Cambridge
January, 2012

ASSIGNMENTS

The following tasks aim to help you think through the debate surrounding population and migration and provide a better understanding of the topic.

1 Brainstorm to find out what you know about population growth. What are the key demographic factors which affect growth?

2 'It took all of human history to reach a world population of 1.6 billion at the beginning of the 20th century. Just one hundred years later, in 2000, the population total had reached 6.1 billion.' Create an illustrated timeline to display this population explosion. Include any events from history which would have had an impact on population size: for example, the 'Black Death' and the discovery of penicillin. Your timeline should be historically accurate as well as visually appealing.

3 Read *Population and human development: the key connections* on pages 5-7. Design a spider diagram on a sheet of A2 paper which clarifies the relationship between the human population and the environment. Include all relevant issues, such as food production and the job market.

4 Read *Most think UK population 'too high'* on page 10. Carry out a survey of your class to find out how other students feel about the size of the UK population. Do they think it is too high? What factors do they think have had the most influence on population size? Design a set of questions to gather opinions on the topic, then display your results as a set of graphs. Try to include at least ten respondents in your survey.

5 Write a letter to your student newspaper arguing that the pressure on the planet is not from rapid population growth, but from over-consumption of natural resources. You will need to support your argument with evidence, informing readers of how lifestyles in developed countries demand over-use of natural resources.

6 Design a leaflet promoting contraception for women living in developing countries. Birth control may not be an accepted part of their culture or faith in the same way that it is for women in many western countries, so your leaflet will need to be presented sensitively.

7 Imagine you have recently moved to a new country with the aim of finding a better job. However, you are still relatively unfamiliar with the language of your new home and it is much harder than you expected to find work. Write a diary entry exploring how you feel about your situation. Would you still be hopeful and optimistic? Or would you feel homesick? How would you go about looking for work?

8 Why might population forecasts sometimes be inaccurate? How are they calculated?

9 Read *David Cameron launches immigration crackdown* on page 30. Do you agree with the Prime Minister's proposed policies on immigration? Will they work? What are the advantages and disadvantages of the plans Mr Cameron has put forward? Discuss the immigration issue in pairs.

10 Design a 'Britishness' questionnaire which could be given to potential UK citizens. Would you test only their English language skills, or their knowledge of Britain and its culture too? Swap questionnaires with someone else in your class and fill in theirs while they attempt yours. Would you both pass?

11 Population Matters is an educational charity which campaigns for a sustainable global population. Visit their website at www.populationmatters.org. What sort of work does the charity do? Do you find their site useful? Write a short review evaluating the site's effectiveness and ease of use.

12 Use Google to find some of the questions from the 'Life in the UK' citizenship test (or view them on *The Guardian*'s website at this URL: www.guardian.co.uk/uk/blog/quiz/2011/oct/11/uk-citizenship-test-quiz). Try and answer as many of the questions as you can. Would you pass the test? Do you think it is too hard, or too easy?

13 Find out what happens at a citizenship ceremony. Who are these ceremonies for, and what is their purpose? Do you think they are a good idea? Come up with a plan for an alternative citizenship ceremony which you think would make new citizens feel both welcome in Britain and proud to be a part of our society.